# FROM DARKNESS
## TO LIGHT

# From Darkness to Light

Danielle Sparacio

**To order additional copies of this book, contact:**
Xlibris Corporation
1-888-795-4274
www.Xlibris.com
Orders@Xlibris.com
95555

# CONTENTS

Acknowledgments .................................................................................9

Chapter One         My Childhood .....................................................11
Chapter Two         Developing Too Fast............................................14
Chapter Three       My Childhood Christmas and Easter...................16
Chapter Four        Junior High School..............................................18
Chapter Five         High School Years ...............................................21
Chapter Six          My Sweet Sixteen ................................................23
Chapter Seven       Trauma during High School................................25
Chapter Eight       Beauty Pageants...................................................28
Chapter Nine        College Applications............................................30
Chapter Ten         My First Love......................................................32
Chapter Eleven      College Life .........................................................34
Chapter Twelve     My Pregnancy......................................................37
Chapter Thirteen    Giving Birth .......................................................40

Photographs as a child.........................................................................42

Chapter Fourteen    College Final Exam Day (Back to College)...........52
Chapter Fifteen     Horror Wedding..................................................54
Chapter Sixteen     College Summer Break (2002) .............................56
Chapter Seventeen   A Chemical Imbalance ........................................58
Chapter Eighteen    Researching My Diagnosis ..................................62
Chapter Nineteen    My Accomplishments...........................................64
Chapter Twenty     Moving from NYC Back to Long Island..............66
Chapter Twenty-one   My Grandma Passed Away ...................................68
Chapter Twenty-two   Divorced..............................................................71
Chapter Twenty-three   A Letter to My Son .............................................73
Chapter Twenty-four   Epilogue...............................................................76

Afterword..............................................................................................79

Dedicated to my son; my grandma, Josephine; my mother; my therapist, Laura; and my lawyer.

# ACKNOWLEDGMENTS

I would like to thank all of my college professors who have inspired and encouraged me. Without them, I never would have completed my education. You have inspired me to aim high with my goals, and never give up. Thanks especially to Gary, Farrell, Judith, Donald, Joyce, Joel, and Ginny. I would like to thank School of Visual Arts for a great education. Malcolm Forbes quoted, "The purpose of education is to replace an empty mind with an open one."

To my mother and grandma, Josephine, who taught me to stay strong and be competitive. My grandma, who loved working seven days a week and spoiling my son and me, and New York City luxury cab transportation! And the art museums and art galleries! And the beautiful New York City clothing stores! Grandma, I miss you every day.

To my loving son, someday you will remember and say, "My mom struggled and sacrificed everything. She always made sure I had clothes, shelter, and food in my belly. She always took me to my sports games." You will always be my special boy and a remarkable son. I love you.

To my therapist, Laura, you showed me how to overcome my fears, ignore malicious people, and keep striving for my goals. I learned to never give up; keep fighting despite a diagnosis of a brain disease. Thank you being a good advocate for me and helping put together important letters for my son's education and my medical insurance. I wish you Laura much success in your career as a therapist. Stay healthy, strong, and keep smiling. Laura, you are a beautiful person inside and out.

Thank you to the staff at the Farmingville Mental Health Clinic for your dedication and perseverance in helping people with mental health issues.

New York City was a wonderful living experience. I loved the culture diversity. I was fortunate to have an outstanding Grandma living in New York City. I would like to thank the doormen at 215 East Ninety-fifth Street,

Luxury Apartments, for carrying up my artwork and packages. I also loved taking luxury cabs to college. Okay, so I was spoiled a lot by my fabulous Grandma, but now I live in a reality world.

Thanks to my son's doctors for helping me with my son's medical conditions, therapy sessions, your encouragement, being a good advocate, and being there for us.

To my best friend Debra: I want you to know how truly grateful I am to have you in my life. Through your encouragement and telephone conversations has helped me to write this book quicker. Debra, you are always in my heart. We laugh and cry together through similar chaotic experiences. We never have boring conversations and jump from one story to the next. I love you and your family always.

To Trudy and Debbie: I want you to know that I treasure our love and friendship. You both are more like a family. Thank you for all your encouragement and support through my good and bad times. You are always there for me, whether it is on the phone or visiting me. I will always love you both.

To my dad: Even though the hard times we have been through in the past, I will always love you, even though you were overprotective of me. You were a good provider for us and tried your best as a dad. You were a hard worker at the post office in Hicksville, New York. You were good at volunteering, helping Veterans like yourself. I will always remember each summer season how we went strawberry picking together as a family. I will always remember our trips together as a family to Washington DC and Florida. I remember when I was working for a catering hall when I was sixteen years old and coming out late from work. Every weekend, I would treat you out to eat at the diner. There is no perfect person in this world, but you have done a wonderful job, Dad. I wish you were still alive to see all my accomplishments and see your grandchild.

To my lawyer: Thank you so much for the emotional support and listening to me on the phone. Thank you for all your help through my divorce process and guidance to remain a strong person. Thank you for being a caring person toward my son and me. There is no lawyer better than you.

*To the people who made fun of me. Thank you for calling me by terrible names and making me cry and making my self-esteem go down. It did not stop me from writing this book and achieving my goals. It does not matter how many friends you have, but you cannot pick your family.*

# CHAPTER ONE

## My Childhood

I was born on October 5, 1979, in New York. My mother told me that I was a colic baby. My parents would take different shifts getting up for me at night. My mother was a stay-at-home mom. My father worked for the post office, and started as a mechanic and moved up to almost supervisor. Before getting cancer at the age of fifty, my father worked as a shop steward and had to retire early.

Life did not get any easier for me growing up. When I was three years old, I became very sick and almost died. To this day, I can still visualize the hospital room. I called the doctor "man." My mother held me in her arms. I had IV hook into my arm.

"What was wrong with me when I was three years old?" I asked my mother.

"It was salmonella. Salmonella is a type of food poisoning. It might have happened when we ate chicken. You had diarrhea, fever, and stomach pain. You were treated in the hospital for a week. I thought I was going to lose you," said my mother.

At the age of four, I went to a private preschool on Long Island. I was very shy in school. I cried on the first day of school. I was glued to my mother's side. She walked me inside school. It took me time to warm up. During playtime, I played with blocks in the corner by myself. I created huge buildings like New York City. I was in my own happy world. I also played with the Fisher-Price kitchen set. I pretended to cook and take care of the baby dolls. I pretended to feed the baby dolls and put them to sleep. The private school made up an award for "being in the kitchen like a mom." I felt proud. I loved painting art in preschool. Snack time was my favorite time. We had buttered cookies and apple juice. We only received two cookies each; I wanted more cookies. I never understood there was a limited amount of drinks and food because of funds.

Growing up as a child was tough. I had a father who was strict. He was a Vietnam veteran, SP4. It was either listen to his orders or else. My father always yelled in the house. He was never a violent person. My parents were strict and did not let me go over friends' houses. The outside world was mysterious to me. It is like putting someone into a bubble and not knowing what is outside in the world.

I started drawing at the age of three. My first drawings were Miss Piggy abstract like the artist Pablo Picasso. I always knew that I wanted to become an art teacher from my young age. I drew a picture on my mother's bedroom wall of a boat and myself inside steering through wavy water. I loved to use my imagination in art.

In elementary school, I was shy. During recess, I played by myself. I could not stand when I never got to the swings first. I stayed by the teacher aides or sat in the cement tunnels on the playground. The playground was dull and boring in the 1980s.

Socially, I never knew how to make friends. I would come home crying. It stinks to be alone and not fitting in. My mother would play with me, but that was not enough. We read books together, built buildings with my colored Legos, and played with my dolls. My books and toys were my best friends. I also played a lot with my clown jack-in-the-box; I loved winding it up listening to the music.

I said to my mother, "I have no friends for a playdate."

My mother would hug me. She tried to understand, but she really didn't.

When I was seven years old, I was on a baseball team. It was a boy's team. My position in baseball was shortstop. Every time, I hit the ball, it went to third base. I liked being the only girl on the team because I like competition and how boys play rough. At the end of the season, I received a trophy.

In school, my fourth-grade year, children would always tease me. They called me by awful names, and it was hurtful. It felt like a dagger to my heart. I never talked to any teacher about this issue. I always looked down at the floor, painfully shy with no confidence.

"You are a sped," the children said.

Feeling hurt inside—waiting to go home and release the tears—I hid in my room, blast the music, and cried. Being in special education classes for two years helped me grow as an individual. My teachers helped me get out of special education in fifth grade. I was in that particular class because of my shyness and low reading level. My teachers told my parents that I did not belong in those classes. The following year, I went into regular classes.

One day, in fifth grade, I was coming home from school off the bus. A small dog chased me as the bus was in motion. I was almost hit by the bus. This issue went straight to the school psychologist the next morning. I was afraid of dogs. I could have been killed and ran over.

My mother screamed, "Oh my god, Danielle."

The next morning, my teacher had me go down to the school psychologist's office. It was a small room with a desk and two chairs. The psychologist pulled out an inkblot cards. I was an artistic person.

I said, "I see images of flowers, butterflies, and pretty things."

I started to look out the window next to watch the birds fly. I found nature and birds interesting. The psychologist yelled at me. I started to cry and could not catch my breath. He handed me a tissue. I wiped the tears away from my brown eyes. I felt nervous and scared of the school psychologist. All I remember was, the school psychologist had a brown mustache and was round like a parachute.

I said, "I see nothing just inkblots."

The psychologist whispered a word "delusional" to another psychologist. I did not understand the word and why both psychologists were arguing. The psychologist dropped the issue. I never told this to my mother until I started writing this book.

# Chapter Two

## Developing Too Fast

Being, almost, the only girl in fifth-grade class made me feel awkward. I was wearing a training bra. Every day, I had chest pains and stomach pains. It was unbearable, felt like a heart attack. I felt like I was going to die.

My mother took me to the doctors. I hated waiting in the waiting room. It took fifteen minutes, and then the receptionist called me in.

The doctor said, "You are blossoming like flowers."

I felt upset and cried. It was insulting. I did not understand why my body was going through these changes. My mother never spoke about this issue. My breasts were huge like Mt. Everest. It was embarrassing. I went to school with baggy shirts to hide my breasts.

One day, in school during fifth grade, the class watched a cartoon about boys and girls bodies developing. I did not understand the video about menstruation, developing, and sex. All I remember is a cartoon character of a man and women in a bathtub kissing. It was strange and confusing. I was naive and innocent. Feeling embarrassed, my teacher knew that I did not understand.

My teacher said, "If you have any questions, you can see the school nurse."

Boys in my class laughed at me when the teacher talked to me. My eyes watered up. My mother never answered any questions about developing, or the birds and the bees and the flowers and the trees. Boys and girls talked slang about developing and sex. I did not even know what sixty-nine meant until I was nineteen years old. Sixty-nine is when two people are having oral sex together in a symmetric way. Gross-out!

When I came home from school, I had to go to the bathroom. I started bleeding down below. I was scared and screamed for my mother. I was crying. I was puzzled. What a hell is this!

My mother said, "You are a woman, now. It is your period."

What was I supposed to do jump up for joy! I did not understand why I was bleeding. My mother handed me an ultrathin Kotex. It was mysterious to me. Blood was gooey and gross. It reminded me of a drink called Bloody Mary. What a description! I was lucky to bleed only for two days lightly. Some women get their period for six to seven days. Being a woman is not easy. A good description in code terms for a period is "The Red Stop Light."

Menstruation—it is uterine bleeding that happens at the end of puberty in girls. Sometimes first periods start at age eleven or thirteen. Menstruation begins two years after girls begin developing breasts, growing pubic and underarm hair. Menstruation continues until menopause, which starts around the age of fifty when monthly menstrual cycle ends. It temporarily stops during pregnancy. Aren't we women lucky!

While developing, in fourth grade, I also experimented shaving my eyebrows and legs. I was not sure how to get skinny looking eyebrows like my mother. I took one of my father's new shavers, and somehow I shaved my eyebrows almost off. I was not aware of the procedure how to get skinny eyebrows. My mother yelled at me because the next day was my school pictures. My mother told me she goes to a salon for her eyebrows. The salon tweezes them and waxes it. What a painful procedure!

The next day, I went to school to take my school pictures. I wore a pink floral skirt and matching shirt. My teacher asked about my eyebrows.

I said, "I shaved my eyebrows to make them skinny like my mother."

My teacher laughed and told me she did the same thing when she was younger. I wanted to look perfect and beautiful.

# CHAPTER THREE

## My Childhood Christmas and Easter

I was so naive as a child in the fourth grade. The children in class laughed at me because I believed in Santa Claus and the Easter Bunny. I wore Christmas shirts and gave my teachers holiday presents. During Easter, my mother bought me bunny ears to wear to school. I was very much into the Christmas and Easter spirit.

Some mean boy had me in tears. "Your parents are Santa Claus."

The teacher told the mean boy, "Quiet."

Santa was real and magical to me. I thought Santa rides his sleigh with reindeers and travel around the world. Every Christmas, I left milk and chocolate chip cookies, which I baked for Santa. The next morning, Santa would leave an empty plate with crumbs. The cup of milk was always full. My mother would say Santa was on a diet and the milk went sour. There were written notes left for me in the morning. I thought, Santa wrote them. I found out my parents worked hard to keep my beliefs alive.

We had a beautifully decorated artificial Christmas tree. It had gold garland, lights, and glass ornaments. On Christmas morning, I opened my presents. My mother took lot of pictures of me. My Grandma gave me a small piece of coal as a joke. As an Italian tradition, we ate lasagna, antipasto, stuffed mushrooms, salad, garlic bread, and artichokes. My mother's cooking was fabulous.

The night before Easter, my grandma, Josephine; my mother; and I dyed Easter eggs. We colored them pink, purple, yellow, blue, and red. One Easter, as a child, I dyed my grandma's legs green as a joke. She laughed, and we had a great time together as a family. Growing up, I was told the Easter bunny hopped through my front door when I was sleeping. The Easter bunny left plastic eggs with jellybeans inside, and I would look for them all over our house. There was a large grass basket with toys and candy inside. I left carrots, veggie dip, and a drink out for the Easter bunny. My mother always took pictures of me during Easter. Every Easter dinner, we had cooked ham with pineapples, applesauce, salad, and antipasto. My mother and I still dye Easter eggs together. My beliefs were shattered by that mean boy in my fourth-grade class, again.

# Chapter Four

## Junior High School

Starting junior high at the age of twelve was nerve-wrecking. My mother made me take a big bus that stopped in front of our house and that was embarrassing. It was hard getting up in the morning at 7:00 a.m. The bus was full of rowdy students, smoking cigarettes and smoking pot in the back of the bus. All the front seats were taken. I would squeeze my skinny butt cheek on the edge of a seat. The bus was loud, listening to the 1980s music. I wish I had earplugs, and the students sang loud on the way to school each day. It gave me headaches.

I was in regents classes. Switching classes was a stressful pain in the ass, not to mention having a regular locker and a gym locker. I only used a gym locker. It was hard remembering different locker combinations, and I always wrote my combo on my left hand. There were A-days and B-days, meaning every other day was gym or enrichment class. It was confusing in the beginning. I carried all my books to each classroom. What a day!

Everyday, I came to school in a designer clothing my grandma, Josephine, bought me in New York City. She took me to Manhattan to go on an expensive shopping spree. I felt like a spoiled princess. I had different outfits each day with different matching shoes. My mother would get my hair done every other week and my nails, too. I had matching hairclips and bows for each outfit. I wore earrings, too. I felt stylish.

This is when shit happened! My grades were Bs and As like a dedicated academic student. I was on the track and cross-country team. I was one of the best runners. The boys hate when I beat them in a running race. They gave me the ugliest look. It did not bother me. I loved running. I used to run three miles a day in junior high.

My favorite classes were art classes, gym classes, and home economics classes. In Home Economics, I learned how to bake cookies and make pretzels. The class ate the cookies and pretzels. I also learned how to sow a toy-stuffed bunny. I received an A on the assignment. I loved learning new things. My teachers liked me. I was a quiet girl in school and stayed to myself.

Girls would get envious of my clothing. They would stare at me and make nasty comments.

The girls said, "Who do you think, you are so rich. You look like a little girl. Do you think you are better than everyone?"

The girls pushed me into the lockers. They ganged up on me in groups, pulling my bows out of my hair. I wore my hair like a little girl. I dealt with being tormented every day. They threatened me not to come on the bus, or they will beat me up. I walked two miles home from school in the rain and the snow. My mother and father were both working at that time. I cried inside my bedroom and created many artworks to release the pain. I turned up my music very loud.

In school, the girls yelled, "You are a slut. You win on the track team by your long nose. You are a cowgirl. Where is your horse?"

I remained silent and never answered them. I never kissed a guy during that time. I was a quiet virgin. There was an amazing guy named Chuck who was an eighth grader that I had a crush on, but I never told him. I never tried to pursue it. I would see him in the school halls going to class wearing his football uniform. He was a handsome Italian guy with a goatee, and smoked a lot.

I concentrated hard in training for winning my track and cross-country races. The girls called me a cowgirl because of my Western outfits with fringes. They were mean and jealous girls.

I came home begging my parents to have me transfer to another junior school. My grades dropped to Bs and Cs. I could not concentrate in school. I was almost thrown into a big locker with the door closed inside. I could not take the torment anymore. I wanted to die at that point. The only outlet was to starve myself. I collapsed numerous times. I felt depressed and lonely with no friends. I was falling apart, and became anorexic.

My mother took me to see a therapist when I was twelve years old. The therapist guided my mother to meet with the school and ask them to transfer to another school. At first, the school refused, but when my father talked about pressing charges, they agreed to transfer me.

I dealt with tormenting in school for two years. It was awful. The girls came on my parents' property, wanting to beat me up. My parents wanted to call the police, but they would not help.

The girls yelled, "Come out, so I can give you a black eye."

They stood outside a long time and finally left. I hid inside my house, scared. My mother felt awful inside for me.

In 1992, in eighth grade, my parents finally had transferred me to another school. My father drove me to school. It would be a new fresh start, but I was still nervous. I was considered "the new girl" in eighth grade. I was still a shy girl. I concentrated on my academics and received As, Bs, and B+s. I felt happy. I was so involved with yearbook club. I was the yearbook artist. I enjoyed drawing pictures for the yearbook and helping laying out the pictures. I spent my lunch period helping the librarian.

I had many favorite classes during my eighth-grade year. In music class, I enjoyed listening to classical music and taking notes based on music. I used to hate when students where rude to the music teacher and made her cry. My heart would go out to her, and I felt sad how disrespectful some students were acting. I was always respectful, all the time.

I also enjoyed technology class, and the teacher was a nice person. I liked learning how to use the power tools, and I built a bridge out of wood and glue. It took about a month to construct my bridge.

Spanish class was interesting and fun to learn to speak. I earned a B+ in that class. At the end of the year, we had a fiesta and hit a piñata in class with a bat and candy fell all over the classroom. The teacher was very nice and gave extra help during her lunchtime. She was a dedicated and devoted Spanish teacher to her students.

At the end of eighth grade, I got voted for best artist. I felt happy, inside, and honored. During my junior high awards night, I received a best artist pin and a science award pin. I was surprised and thanked my teachers. I really worked hard in school. I loved school and learning.

I really was not interested in boys during junior high. I did not have sex, yet either. I never tried smoking and never took drugs. The school bathrooms always smelled; it needed more than Lysol. I always went to the bathroom either at home or in the school nurse's office.

Through years of therapy, it was hard to forget the torment I went through in sixth and seventh grades. I felt as though my body image must be perfect. I continued to diet, eating one meal a day. I wanted to be like famous celebrities and top models on the runway.

During spring 1994, I had to run a cross-country race in junior high school for gym class. The gym teacher was giving out trophies for the top nine runners. I was craving to win a trophy. I strived for it. I did not eat that particular day. Toward the end of the race, I slowed down and almost collapsed. Out of approximately two hundred runners, I received a ninth-place trophy. I was happy and showed my parents when I got home from school. I still have my running trophy.

# CHAPTER FIVE

## High School Years

I started high school in September 1994, at the age of fifteen. I was nervous and getting anxiety. I had new teachers, and the school was bigger. I was scared what to expect. There were cliques, jocks, the cheerleaders, and the popular students. I did not fit into any group. I was a quiet virgin who stayed by myself. Every day, I walked to my classes alone. Mainly, I concentrated on my regents classes and on achieving high grades. I wanted to be in Honor Society and in all clubs.

I went to the library on my lunch break. I studied and did my homework in the library. I was a bookworm nerd. I skipped lunch every day to remain a size zero in juniors.

One day, in the library, a blond guy approached me in the library. He sat across from me. I felt nervous. He was six foot and skinny like a twig. He wore metal glasses and black jeans. He was a stranger to me and very odd.

I was busy doing my math regents homework. The blond guy pulled out a small bag out of his pocket. It looked blackish, green like Italian cooking herbs mashed up. I started to get nervous and shaking. My eyes tear up. My parents never talked about drugs.

I said, "What is that?"

He said, "Drugs. Pot. It will make you feel good. If you tell anyone, I will come after you."

I refused it and started to cry. The blond guy darted out the library fast. He never bothered me again.

Throughout my high school years, I was in Honor Society with a high GPA. I was in French cooking club, Future Teacher's of America Club,

National Art Honor Society, and Environmental Club. I helped with different fundraisers in school.

Each year, the high school had senior citizen proms for elderly people. There was a DJ. The students danced with the elderly. I helped to serve the lasagnas and salads. Clean up was not fun! I did enjoy helping the elderly people and seeing their smiling faces.

I also helped, each year, building a house for Habitat for Humanity through the school. It was a nice learning experience. I hammered siding on the house. I enjoyed myself donating my time. I also hammered beams within the house, too. We stayed there a couple of hours and ate our bagged lunch there.

Every day, for four years, I walked by myself to my high school classes because I was timid. I was an outcast, never got into any trouble, and stayed by myself. In my senior year, I drove myself to school in a black Blazer. For three years, my father always drove me to school before going to work. I was grateful.

# CHAPTER SIX

## My Sweet Sixteen

On October 5, 1995, I turned sixteen. I felt premonitions that my father was going to die.

My father said quietly to his adopted mother, "I was exposed to asbestos for years at my job."

I did not understand what my father was saying. I never heard of that word before. I never bothered to research it either. My father and his adopted mother grew quiet.

I begged my parents for a sweet sixteen party. I was afraid time was ticking seeing my father. The preparations were overwhelming. We went to only one catering hall and booked it quickly. My parents and my grandma went half to pay for my sweet sixteen party. I was very grateful. My mother bought the Hawaii decorations and balloons. We choose buffet-style food and fancy Italian cookies. We also had a DJ. My mother took me to a fancy dress shop. I bought a bright pink sequin dress. I wanted to be like a princess for one day. My mother took me to a salon to get my hair done.

It was 5:30 p.m., and I rushed to get ready for my big night. My stockings ripped, and lucky, I bought a spare. I had trouble zippering up my dress in the back, not to mention two-eye hooks were behind my neck. I put on my light blue eye shadow and pink lipstick.

I cried to my parents, "It starts at 6:00 p.m. We are going to be late. I wish I had a limo to take me to the catering hall. I am going to be embarrassed being driven inside a reddish station wagon."

My father said, "Be happy that you are having a sweet sixteen party."

Finally, twenty minutes later, we arrived at the catering hall. We had to put our decorations up fast and the balloons on each table. My black satin shoes with heels were already aching my feet. The catering hall was short staffed with waitress. There were no busboys to help these young waitresses. At the end of my party, my grandma tipped the waitresses a hundred dollars. The tables were always cleaned and organized.

I loved the music the DJ was playing. The DJ had some speaker trouble. My father, my family, and I danced all night. My father asked my mother to dance with him. She rejected him because she was shy to dance in front of people. During dancing, I was getting annoyed how my dress became unbearable. I changed into another outfit and took off my shoes. I started to break dance and do flips. I danced in the middle of the floor by myself with my family clapping. It was fun and a blast. I liked being the center of attention. My favorite songs were "Hand's up" and "The Electric Slide." My father and I slow danced to "Sixteen Candles." It was unforgettable. I was timid. I never slowed danced before.

My father said, "Follow my steps or just put your feet on top of mine."

The DJ announced, "How cute. She dances like her dad." My dad put up the middle finger and the DJ laughed.

The lights went dim. My cake was rolled out on a table with candles lit. I felt a little timid at first. My family sang "Happy Birthday." My grandma was so happy for me. She stood by me, clapping and smiling. I had a special cake designed, and my family laughed. My sweet sixteen cake had a cartoon character of a muscle man in underwear. My family took pictures of me around my cake. I cut the first slice of strawberry and banana cake. It tasted delicious.

I opened my presents at the catering hall. My grandma gave me a money tree, too. She gave me a charm saying "Queen Bee." I opened another present from my grandma; it was double-boxed and taped-up good. It was a piece of coal, a Halloween toy rat, and then a sexy satin gown for bedtime.

My family laughed and they yelled, "Is this a bachelorette party?"

I was not sure what they meant by this. I received a lot of money, jewelry, and clothing. My sweet sixteen was unforgettable.

I said to my grandma, "Why did you give me a rat and a piece of coal?"

My grandma said, "When you are mean at times, you can be a spoiled brat."

My mom told my grandma laughing, "That is your granddaughter. You spoiled her, not me."

It was 11:00 p.m. The night came to an end, and I enjoyed my sweet sixteen. It was one unforgettable party. I danced with my father before he passed away. It was a meaningful memory for me. I have pictures to remember always that moment. I went to sleep fast that night.

# CHAPTER SEVEN

## Trauma during High School

Around December 1996, my father was suffering from cancer. He started out with body aches and flu-like symptoms. He went for various testing and blood tests. My father went for treatment at a hospital. Seeing my father, as months went by, destroyed me. He was losing his hair at the age of fifty. He looked like an old man. His hair turned gray fast. His body weight dropped a lot. My mother was always crying, and I never talked to her about the situation. The doctors came from the hospital room and talked to my mother.

The doctor said, "Your husband has six months to live."

I overheard what the doctor told my mother. I waited in the hallway. I broke down and cried.

I said constantly, "No . . . No . . ."

My mother demanded that my father remain in our house and get treated. It was difficult seeing my father weak and helpless in bed. I had to help take care of my father. I helped to feed my father and change his clothing.

My mother was constantly working at a nearby nursing home to help financially. She worked sixteen-hour shifts a day. She paid for our house and other expenses. My job was to help watch over my father. I had to quit my waitress job to be with my father. I worked as a waitress for two years and loved my job.

I had a lot of pressure on me. I had to keep a high GPA, remain in my after-school clubs, National Honor Society, and National Art Honor Society. I also had to cancel my class trip to London and Paris. I used the excuse, financial reasons, and never spoke about my father dying.

On November 1, 1997, I spoke to my father while he was suffering in pain.

My father was crying, "Danielle, I know you will go to college. You will become an art teacher, one day. You are always smart. I love you."

I said, "Dad, are you going to my graduation?"

My father cried and did not answer me. During that night, I heard my father yell my name as he was in pain. I saw his eyes roll up and then down. My mother came into the bedroom. She called 911 for help. She explained on the phone whispering, "My husband died from cancer." I could hear my mother crying. I cried in my bed with the blankets over my head.

My father died on November 2, 1997, on All Saints' Day. I was supposed to go to school that day. I called up my school guidance counselor, and missed two days of school. My guidance counselor was very supportive emotionally when my father died. Some of my teachers went to my father's wake. I felt empty and robbed; my father died too young.

I went back to school, two days later. I felt as though everyone was staring at me in my creative writing class. I wrote a poem about my father in creative writing class and read it out loud in class. I started to stutter as I read my poem.

# *Faith*

A simple tear shed from her face,
I do not know where I am going from place to place.
My head is spinning round and round.
My poor dear father is constantly in my thoughts.
He is dying of cancer with six months to live.
It is shocking, but hard to believe.
Until that time comes, then I will react.
Otherwise, I have faith in my father and in God.

The class was silent. I started to cry. The teacher handed me a sympathy card. That did not make me feel any better, but it was nice they thought of me. One guy came up to me and stated his father recently died, too. I just wanted to be alone.

I spoke to my guidance counselor how I wanted to drop out of high school. I felt torn apart; I wanted my father alive. The guidance counselor encouraged me to complete my education and remain strong.

On June 1998, I did graduate high school. It was a sunny day. I received an Honor Society Medal. I felt honored and good inside. I worked hard through my struggles. My ranking was near the top 50 percent out of 210 graduates. My mother watched me at graduation. I really wished my father was still alive to see my graduation, too. I knew my father was in heaven above, like my angel, watching over me.

On my high school graduation day, my mom and I went to visit my dad's grave. I kept on my graduation white cap and gown. I wore my medal, too. My mother gave me a dozen of roses for my graduation. I placed them by my father's gravestone. I could feel the wind blow, and it was a little chilly. My father probably was looking above me in heaven and crying tears of happiness. Going to my father's gravesite was depressing. In 1998, it was the last time I visited my father's gravesite.

# CHAPTER EIGHT

## Beauty Pageants

In 1998, I entered into two beauty pageants. It was at a hotel in Long Island. We had to show up an hour ahead of time. I had to check in at a table where pageant girl's names were on a list. There had to be a parent present if one was underage. My mother had me wear my dress from my sweet sixteen. I wore a size zero at that time. My mother would get my hair done in curls with a clip on one side. I wore pink lipstick and light blue eye shadow. I put a little blush on, too.

I entered into modeling and photogenic competitions. I received a trophy for "most photogenic" face. I loved getting my pictures taken and modeling on the runway. Personal video cameras were forbidden inside the beauty pageants. I wanted to be beautiful and that perfect size. I was never happy with my body image, even wearing a size zero. My dream was to be a professional model.

I participated in a second beauty pageant. My mother and I shopped at an exclusive dress shop. We bought a purple gown with sequins on the top. Going into beauty pageant competitions, there is a lot of pressure and stress. Girls are catty, gossip, and criticize each other. I just wanted to feel beautiful and be like top models on television.

In competition, pageant judges asked questions like: what you want to do in your future, what school activities do you participate in, what types of volunteer activities do you do, etc. Sometimes, I froze up like a scared deer in headlights. Then, I warmed up and answered the questions using proper grammar. Parents snickered and have smirks on their faces. I ignored their rudeness.

At the end of the competition, the pageant judges came to their conclusion. Different girls were called up for their trophy. I felt like trash. I thought I was not getting anything. I came as runner-up and received a trophy. I felt happy, again. I outgrew doing beauty pageants at nineteen.

While doing research, the first beauty pageant that occurred was in 1985. The beauty pageant had dogs, men, and women based on physical beauty. In beauty pageants, there is modeling, talent show, interviews, bikini contests, and photogenic competitions.

# Chapter Nine

## College Applications

I decided to go away to college in New York City. My grandma, Josephine, lived in New York City. I waited until last minute for applying to colleges because of my father's death. I could not concentrate. I could not stay home on Long Island with my mother. She was always depressed from my father's passing away. I had to move on with my life and had to worry about my future. I applied for Pratt, New York University, Parsons School of Design, and School of Visual Arts.

For my application process, I wanted to pursue a double major in art education and fine arts, bachelor's degree. I had to design a twenty-piece art portfolio, a college essay, have a sketchbook for presentation, a high GPA, and high SAT scores.

It was a stressful process meeting each college for interview. I took my grandma with me during my interviews. I traveled from Long Island to New York City. During my college interviews, I had to speak about my artwork in a formal analysis. A formal analysis is depicting artwork in terms of line, shape, color, and form. I related my artwork to my favorite artist, Pablo Picasso.

After months of waiting for acceptance letters, I felt nervous. I had to figure out which college would give me a good education and a scholarship. The waiting process was stressful. My decision was to go to School of Visual Arts. I sent out an acceptance letter to School of Visual Arts and thanked them. The other colleges, I did not accept their offer.

The financial aid department of School of Visual Arts was very helpful and accommodating. I applied for financial aid. The financial aid form was complex. I was very nervous how much financial aid I would receive. I did not want to get stuck with a huge college loan.

There was a long waiting process for financial aid. I was anxious for the financial aid results. My grandma always kept me calm. Finally, I received a letter in the mail; I received grant scholarships, SADD scholarship, POW/MIA scholarship, and School of Visual Arts Merit scholarship for four years.

My grandma was a big part of the reason going to college in New York City. She promised to pay for any transportation expenses and my summer classes. The summer classes were not covered by my scholarships or financial aids. My grandma was my "hero," encouraging with everything I did in life. If it was not for my grandma, I would have never accomplished so much in life. During my stay at my grandma's apartment, she was sweet and accommodating. Every night, my grandma cooked for me and took my clothes to the drycleaner's once a week. There were times we did not see eye to eye because she would smoke her cigarettes in the apartment. I had to tell her to go outside because the smell would make me sick. My grandma always wanted the best from me, and to do well in school. She would brag about me to her coworkers at work about my accomplishments. My grandma had a great smile and had a heart of gold.

# CHAPTER TEN

## My First Love

In June 1998, during the end of my senior year in high school, I started seeing a guy during my college application process. We met in high school. I approached him at the end of June and asked him to come to the prom. He did not come with me. Two days before he left New York, we decided to have a long-distance relationship. I moved to New York City in July 1998.

In July 1998, my boyfriend went into the air force. He promised, once he graduated basic training, he would transfer to Delaware. He would see me every weekend in New York City at my grandma's apartment.

My grandma paid for my boyfriend's transportation to New York City from Delaware every weekend. She helped us financially. My boyfriend and I were in a serious relationship together. I loved him so much. We talked about the future and some day having a son.

One afternoon, I was watching a show on television, *Play Boy*. I really did not understand much about sexual positions or types of birth control. My mother never spoke about sex; it was taboo. I was intrigued by the various positions of sex on television. There were men and women on television on motorcycles screwing. The next scene was a man and woman screwing in the shower.

I thought to myself, I wanted to be exotic and unforgettable with my boyfriend. My boyfriend claimed to be a virgin. That was hard to believe!

My boyfriend came over from Delaware to New York City. I told him how much I missed him. I was deeply in love with him. We decided to make love in the shower. We made out. It felt so good and passionate. He started to get nervous and did not want to drop me down in the shower. He ejaculated inside me. Gross-out! I started to cry, thinking I could wash it away. He told me I will be okay. He left that weekend back to Delaware. I kept that day a secret.

Throughout college, we remained in a relationship together. My boyfriend called me every night and visited me on weekends. My grandma sent my boyfriend phone cards every week to keep in contact.

Each month, I mailed care packages for my boyfriend. I bought him designer clothing and sent some stuffed animals with cute sayings. I also bought him a purple color Blazer car to have transportation to go back and forth from Delaware to New York City. My boyfriend was my real first love, and he ruined it, later on.

# CHAPTER ELEVEN

## College Life

My grandma came with me to college orientation. Orientation was long and boring. It had a lot of informative information about requirements toward our degrees. There were a couple of cute guys in the auditorium. I was puzzled to find were my different classes were located. One blond guy approached me at orientation.

The blond guy said, "Hello, my name is . . ."

I said, "I am Danielle. I am a freshman. My major is art education and fine arts. This is my grandma."

The blond guy said, "Hello . . . Grandma. I am a senior majoring in film."

There was a pause for a minute. The blond guy walked with my grandma, and I around the different college buildings. He seemed friendly, but not my type to date. I was grateful for the tour the blond guy gave me. The blond guy wanted a boyfriend-girlfriend relationship with me, but I told him no. I was very faithful and devoted to my boyfriend, and very much in love with him. I focused all my energy on my relationship with my boyfriend, my college education, and my grandma at that particular time.

The first day of college, September 10, 1998, I was nervous to attend class. My class started at 9:00 a.m. My grandma came with me to the college doors to make me feel comfortable. We traveled in a luxury cab from uptown to downtown Manhattan. I wore a backpack like an innocent schoolgirl.

I said quietly, "Grandma, you can leave, now."

My first class was an English humanities class. I loved Shakespeare, *Othello*, *Macbeth*, writing various papers, and meeting well-known writers. I always sat in the front row near the English professor.

My English professor was a unique well-known writer. She wore pigtails on each side. Some students would say she looked like a shaggy dog. She was nice and helpful with correcting my class work. I learned a lot from my English professor. I also took her creative writing classes, too. She was an inspirational teacher.

On the first day of my English humanities class, I met two nice, quiet guys named Julian and Jay. There were cliques starting. I stayed away from that stuff. Everyday Jay, Julian, and I ate together during our class lunch break. We talked about our writing assignments, artwork, and art shows. Jay and Julian were nice, respectful guys.

Julian went to college with us for a few months and then left. I really liked Julian; he was a gorgeous guy. He wore metal glasses and was clean cut. Julian looked fabulous in jeans. He was sweet like Godiva chocolate. After he dropped out of college in our freshman year, we lost contact.

Jay followed me to each college class everyday like as if he had a crush on me. I snapped at Jay, "Do you like me or something?"

He said, "No, I just wanted to be your friend."

I laughed. "Okay, we can be friends."

Jay and I sat together in all our classes—art history, English humanities, painting, and drawing. We were stuck like glue. Every day, we saved a seat for each other. We competed together with grades and assignments. Jay was like me, almost a straight (A) student. He's well-mannered and has a lot of good qualities.

One day, in my painting class, I wore a black trench coat. I brought a hanger and a plastic bag for my coat. I did not want it to get ruined. I was a clean and neat artist. Other times, I came into class wearing a dress suit, skirts, and cleavage shirts. I wanted to feel beautiful.

Another day, I had a drawing class. I did not know what to expect. The professor took class attendance. Our assignment in class was to draw the model, but he was nude. Jay and I were quiet. My mouth dropped, feeling embarrassed. The model posed close to a girl in our class. The model had a huge penis, probably bigger than my hand. It was uncomfortable drawing nude models at first until I became use to it. Most of my nude drawings look cartoonish and abstract. Every artist has a different style. I love to use acrylic paints, markers, and pencils. I love to use paper better than using a canvas because of storage reasons.

My world art history class was interesting. There were approximately one hundred students in that particular class. We learned how to depict an artwork into a formal analysis. Our assignments were to go to various art exhibitions and write papers on it. We also had to write an assignment about a church in Harlem. I loved visiting the church. On our midterms and final exams, we had to remember the titles of artworks, the dates, and the artists. I loved the challenge and strived for excellence.

My favorite college classes were clinical psychology. Learning about the study of the mind was fascinating and educational. I learned about neurological disorders; for example, schizophrenia, bipolar, ADHD, bulimia, anorexia, ADD, autism, and many other things. I used to take massive notes in clinical psychology classes. I kept my notes as a reference. There was a lot of reading material, and I did additional research for the class that I found inspiring about mental health.

I loved college and learning. Writing papers was my favorite. Getting an education is so important to improve oneself for a better career. At the age of twenty-two and a half, I signed up for a master's degree in fine arts, and I was supposed to get some scholarship money. The only thing that stopped me from getting my master's degree was financial reasons, and I wound up very ill. I had to drop out of CW Post on Long Island. At the age of thirty, I went back for my master's degree in early childhood education birth through second grade on part scholarship. I had a high GPA for grad school.

For my undergraduate, I enjoyed studying until 1:00 a.m., going to the library every day and researching various materials. I also did an internship in New York City through a company working with children at an elementary school. It was hard work. I also did internship as an art teacher twice a week, too. On weekends, I volunteered for Art for Kids at the college. I enjoyed learning different things and various techniques. I was never lazy in college, even at the time of being pregnant. I never complained being pregnant. I never took a maternity leave and never took a break.

I took a science humanities class called animal behavior. It was the funniest class I have ever taken. We watched videos of animals reproducing. We learned about amoebas and protozoa. The professor talked a lot about reproduction and sex. Some of the information was informative while being pregnant. My professor would end the class by saying, "Drink Coke and have protected sex." I wanted to burst out laughing. All the students looked at me. I received a B+ for that class. My mother told me I should have aced that class. I laughed.

In my fourth year of college, I loved the fine arts department. Each student had their own art studio space to create their artwork. I concentrated on creating paintings on canvas based on my life experiences. My acrylic paintings seemed fragmented like puzzle pieces. I loved to experiment with fabrics, paint, watercolors, and markers. My assignment was to write a ten-page bachelor's thesis based on my artwork. I also had to go to lot of art seminars, visit galleries of well-known artist's artwork, and write up papers. Most of the time, I brought my grandma along with me. My grandma was a big part of my life.

# Chapter Twelve

# My Pregnancy

Months passed by, I did not understand why I was not getting my period. I was not gaining weight; I only weighed ninety pounds. It was a confusing situation and I did not understand it. I could not talk to my mother because we were not on good talking terms. She did not want me to be with my boyfriend. I was afraid to tell my grandma.

In my sixth month of being pregnant, I went to my clinical psychology class. My professor took time after class to talk to me every week.

I said, "My period stopped and I do not know what is wrong." I lifted up my shirt half way showing her my belly.

She said, "It can be anything or pregnancy."

I cried. I told her, "I tried to wash out my boyfriend's cum. I did not understand much about pregnancy."

She said, "Did you see a GYN or tell your family?"

I said, "No . . . I am scared to tell my family. I am scared a doctor will call me a slut."

She said, "You should rethink this and go to a GYN doctor."

I called up my mother on Long Island. We talked about college and my good grades. Then, I changed the subject.

I said crying, "I am pregnant, Mom. I am sorry to disappoint you."

My mother cried, "I will look up a GYN doctor for you in New York City." There was silence.

My mother said, "How many months are you pregnant?"

I cried, "I do not know. I am scared being a teenager pregnant."

My mother said, "Don't worry, I will help you. That is what I am here for on this earth."

My mother made a doctor's appointment for me. My grandma, my mother, and I went together to the GYN doctor. I went up to the receptionist's window slowly. I was crying because I was scared.

The receptionist said, "What are you here for?"

I looked down at the carpet and said, "I might be pregnant."

The receptionist looked at me because I was a small ninety-pound teenager. She sighed. It made me feel bad inside and uncomfortable.

I waited in the waiting room for one hour. Finally, I was called inside. I had my mother come inside the room with me. I imagined people would be mean, but it was the opposite. The nurses and doctors wanted to help me. The doctor told me to pee in a cup. I took a sonogram. The doctor asked me questions. I did not understand most of them.

The doctor said, "How many months are you pregnant."

I said crying, "I do not know nor the date. I am scared."

The doctor said, "Do you want to keep the baby? You cannot have an abortion. Do you want to give up your child for adoption? I know a doctor family who can take care of your baby."

I said crying, "I am keeping my son even if I have to struggle raising my baby. I will have to struggle to finish college. I will make it."

The doctor smiled. The doctor explained the purpose of a sonogram. He put gel on my stomach. The doctor moved the device across my stomach. Looking at the sonogram made me cry more. I saw my baby's little body. It looked like a boy.

The doctor announced, "It is a boy. You are six months pregnant. Please make follow-up appointments."

I went to the receptionist window and made my regular appointments as directed. My mother went back to Long Island. My grandma and I returned to her apartment, which was uptown Manhattan.

That night, I called my boyfriend on the phone and told him I was six months pregnant. He kept questioning if it was his. I told him that I was only with him. That is when "hell" broke out. My boyfriend mistreated me and called me by horrible names. He told me it was my fault. It takes two people to make a baby, I was thinking.

Every day, I went to school wearing baggy shirts. I held secrets from my college professors, my family, and my college friends about being a pregnant teenager and being abused by my boyfriend. I was quiet in college. My schedule was packed. I did day, night, weekend college, and did an art teacher internship. I was tired everyday, but somehow made it through my days going to college. I held back my tears from people.

I maintained a 3.5 GPA at School of Visual Arts on scholarship. There were college days, I wish that I could have missed class, but I did not. I refused to be a failure and dropout. I would take my grandma with me to college at night. At first, professors would question me, and I told them I am pregnant. They were shocked. I would hear college students snickering, but it did not bother me. I was there for one reason—an education and earn a degree. It is so easy to judge someone, but we all have feelings and a heart. Everyone has some sort of skeleton in their closet. *No one is perfect.*

# CHAPTER THIRTEEN

## Giving Birth

On March 15, 2000, it was my beginning of my eight month. I had a long day from college, sixteen hours long. I was tired. The bus ride was taking so long from Twenty-third Street to Ninety-fifth Street. I thought I was never going to get to my grandma's apartment. I was not feeling well. I called my grandma on my cell, telling her that I am ready to pass out. A woman stranger saw me on the bus pregnant, ready to pass out. She was so kind and gave me a water bottle, not opened. Finally, I was at my stop, and I ran to my grandma's apartment.

My son was not moving inside my stomach. I called the hospital in New York City. I was told to come in immediately. I did not call an ambulance because I was embarrassed and scared. Grandma called a cab around 2:00 a.m.; the cab drove fast. The streets were empty, and only homeless people were out. I did not know what to expect.

At the hospital, I called my mother and my boyfriend. I was in the waiting room filling out paperwork. I really did not understand the procedure about pregnancy. I became nervous and scared. I was called in, and was transported in a wheelchair to a room. The nurses took my blood pressure and hooked me to a heart monitor for my son and myself. They told me my son's heart rate is down. I had to be induced into labor. I did not understand what that meant. It made me cry, and I did not want my unborn son to die. I was feeling confused, and my heart was torn up.

My mother and my boyfriend showed up three hours later. My mother stayed in the hospital room with me. She requested an epidural for me. Epidural numbs the pain, but hurts when they put the needle in my back. The process was painful and upsetting. I never cried so much in my life.

My pregnancy lasted from 2:00 a.m. to 7:45 p.m. On March 15, 2000, my son was born. The doctors swabbed my son with a Q-tip. I signed papers, not knowing it was a paternity test. I knew my son was my boyfriend's child. I was never with anyone else. I was faithful and devoted to him.

The nurses and doctors said to my boyfriend, "It is your son, too."

I did not know what to name my son. I thought names like Picasso, Michael, Leonardo, and Raphael. If my child was a girl, it would have been either Brittany or Jaime.

After giving birth, my mother gave me a chocolate donut. I was hungry. What a tough day! The doctor had a donut, too. And an hour later, I threw up the donut.

A social worker and the nurse tried to explain how to prepare the formula. I did not understand. I had my mother teach me how to sterilize the bottles and prepare the formula. All I knew is how to bathe my son every day, dressed him up in expensive clothes, feed him, changed his diapers, take him to the doctor's, and put him into his crib for bedtime. I sang to him and read stories to him. *My son is my world.*

On March 16, 2000, my son and I were discharged from the hospital. It was a rainy, windy day. I was afraid the rain would get my son sick. I wanted to stay an extra day in the hospital. My son weighed four pounds and eleven ounces. He was nineteen inches long. He had a big feet, and I was very concerned, too.

The doctor said, "Your son will be a big boy. Maybe, about six foot. He is a healthy baby."

I went home, back home to grandma's apartment. My boyfriend and my relationship were falling apart. He yelled at me and abused me. He called me by names. My boyfriend returned back to Delaware the next day. He kept in contact by telephone and traveled every weekend to see me in New York on my grandma's expense.

# PHOTOGRAPHS AS A CHILD

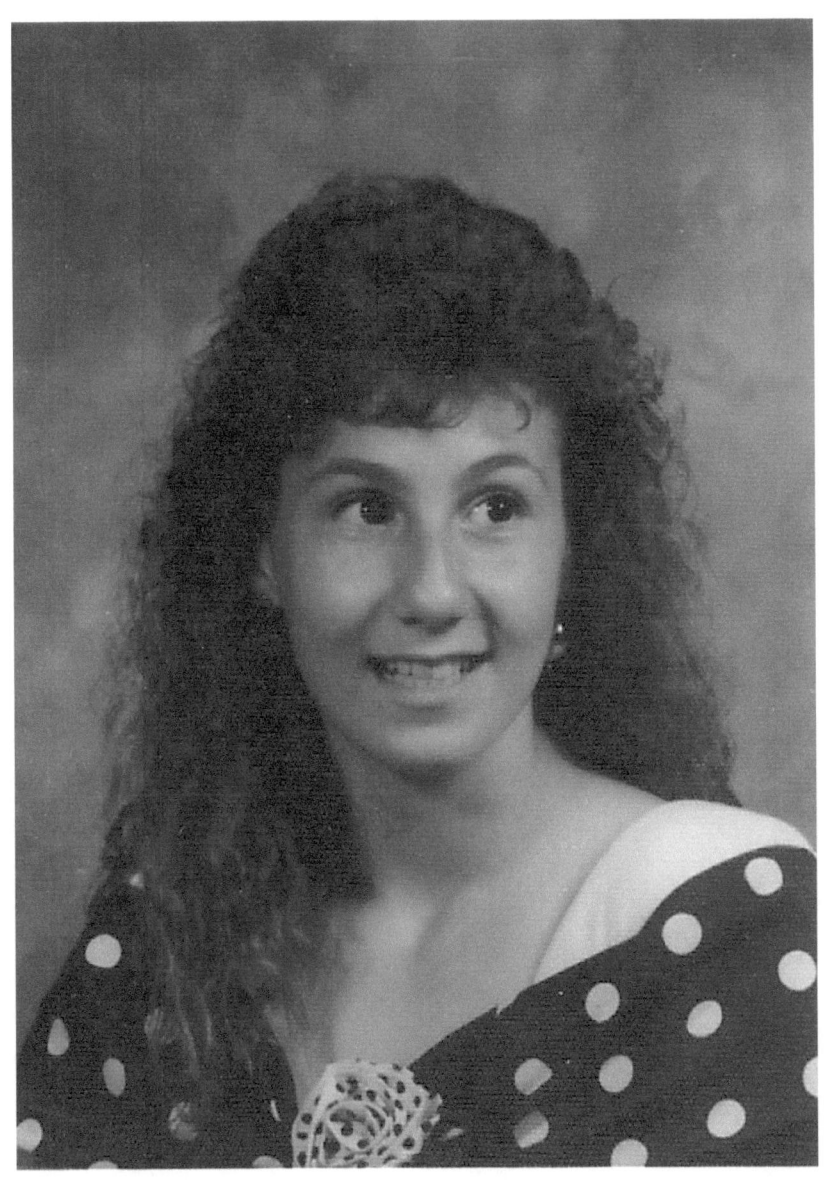

HAMLET WINES

ALL ☆ STAR
1991

# CHAPTER FOURTEEN

## College Final Exam Day
## (Back to College)

On March 17, 2000, I had to return to college for my final exam in Ideas and Art. It was an art history class. I took my son inside in a baby carrier. I was tired and overwhelmed. My period was heavy after giving birth. It was icky. There were tears in my eyes from my hidden secrets. My college professor was shocked to see me back after giving birth. My college friends were surprised to see me. I never gave up.

My professor showed slides of artwork on the wall. We had to name the artist and the time periods. I was well prepared for my final exam, and knew everything. I knew I aced my art history test.

My friend said, "Little Danielle is a mom now."

"Yeah," I said proudly.

During my third and forth year of college, I struggled to go to college. There were so many responsibilities as a parent. My mother and my grandma took turns babysitting while I went to college. My mother's friend Billie helped to babysit my son, too. There were days, I took my son to college with me. I did day school, sometimes night classes. On Friday nights, I went back to Long Island and worked for a European clothing store for the weekends. Spending a lot of time with my son was hard. I did my best to manage everything. I was very tired. I juggled college, worked as a sales associate, worked as an art teacher doing internship, and took care of my son.

I bought my son's clothing, formula, food, and paid for his doctor bills. My boyfriend refused to help. I received help through a program called WIC. WIC helps people who have hardly any money for basic foods like cheese and milk. They also help pay for children's formula. If you need special formula, a doctor has to give you a prescription to give to WIC. I felt embarrassed in the WIC waiting room. There were a lot of pregnant teens asking for help. I never knew there was help in New York for people like me. There was also a place called Planned Parenthood to get help, too. Planned Parenthood helps women, teens, and families who rely on reproductive healthcare, educational programs, and advocacy.

Social Services is another place to get help for yourself, your child, and your family. They can help with housing, food stamps, medical insurance, and possibly as a source for a job referral. It is a long process to go through, just do not give up receiving the help.

I would also recommend not hiding your pregnancy, and seek a GYN immediately to get the help you and your baby deserve. If you are pregnant, make sure you listen to a GYN doctor on how to take the prenatal vitamins. Always drink a lot of milk and water, most of all eat healthy food. Do not either smoke or drink when you are pregnant. I never did any of that.

# CHAPTER FIFTEEN

## Horror Wedding

I thought things would get better for my boyfriend and me. On July 2, 2000, we decided to get married at a catering hall. My son was five months old. I bought my son a black and white preemie tuxedo. He looked adorable. My mother and grandma paid for the wedding. It was a $10,000 wedding. My mother bought me a Victorian-beaded wedding dress for $2,000. I bought a princess crown with a veil. I felt like a magical princess.

At the catering hall, the professional photographers were fabulous. My boyfriend and I posed for various pictures. I felt like a fashion model. I loved pictures being taken of me.

The wedding music started outside near the garden area where we were about to be married. I tear up because my father was not alive to see me get married. At the time, I deeply loved my husband. My husband's family started being ignorant after we exchanged our vows, our rings, and signed the marriage papers. My husband and I opened a white straw box and released a dozen white doves. It was for good luck and great beginning as a "family." I had one bridesmaid, one maid of honor, flower girls, a ring boy, and a best man from my husband's side.

We all went to Cocktail Hour. I loved the fruits, vegetables, the cakes, Italian foods, and drank a nonalcohol strawberry drink. I also had Virgin pina coladas. I mingled with my family and my mother's friends.

My husband's family was beyond rude. They questioned me about my future, my education stats, living arrangements, and money. I walked away and stayed by my mother, my grandma, and my son.

After Cocktail Hour, we were announced into the dining room where the DJ was playing music. The DJ announced my husband's name and mine. There was silence from his family. My family and friends were clapping.

We slow danced to one of Celine Dion's love songs. My eyes tear up because I deeply loved my husband. We slowed danced again, but with our son. It was nice.

Everyone had a choice to eat filet mignon, chicken, or fish. They ate salad, intermezzo, and squid salad. It was an excellent Italian meal. The DJ played an Italian song while eating.

The music stopped playing. It was silent for a couple of minutes. One of my husband's family members grabbed the microphone. I looked up in amazement.

The bald guy said, "If you want to keep your marriage going, keep your mouth shut."

My husband's mother called me by horrible names. I refused to let her hold my son. They cornered me to torment me. My family stopped the situation by taking my son away from my arms from them. I cried. It was a disaster wedding. My husband said nothing and did not stand up to his family. My family was in a shock. A wrecked wedding!

We went back to my mother's house to get ready for our honeymoon the next day. We went to Florida. My grandma paid for our honeymoon and gave me money for spending. My mother watched my son while we went on our honeymoon. We went to Disney, Magic Kingdom, MGM, Universal Studios, Blizzard Beach, and Animal Kingdom.

My husband and I went parasailing in Florida. It was dangerous and daring. I would never do it again. The operator for parasailing has you sign a consent form saying, they are not responsible if you die during parasailing. We took the risk. I was high up in the sky like a parachute being pulled by a boat. Only gravity and a long rope were holding me. If you are a daredevil, try this! I went parasailing for fifteen minutes. It was fun, but I missed my son.

After a seven-day honeymoon trip, I went back to my mother's house to see my son. My husband went back to Delaware. He traveled back and forth to Long Island almost every weekend on my family's expense. I thought being married would make things better. He was my first love.

Eventually, we opened our wedding gifts from my family and some cards. The cards from my husband's family were either empty with no money or had sayings like, "You are a bitch. I hope you get divorced. You are a slut." I cried. I told my husband I will save these cards to show my son when he gets older. My husband ripped them up and threw them in the garbage. He never stood up for us as a "family."

# Chapter Sixteen

## College Summer Break (2002)

I was in my fourth year of college, and it was summer break. I decided not to take classes during this summer and take a break. I deserved one! I would start up again in September 2002, my senior year.

My grandma gave me money to go to Delaware for two weeks when our son was two years old. I thought I would like being with my husband. He was not the same guy I met in high school. He was mysterious and secretive. One night, he was popping pills not prescribed by the doctor. He was also drinking alcohol. I begged him to stop. He did not and hit me. I called my grandma when my husband was sleeping. I was silently crying. My grandma was a lifeline to help me out, financially and emotionally.

Grandma told me on the phone, "I will send you money through the mail and make sure you get there first. If it gets worse, leave fast with your son when he is at work."

The next day became worse. My husband came in the house with muddy shoes and made tracks throughout the kitchen. He grabbed me and a mop. He demanded that I clean the mess in front of my child. I cried. A couple hours later, we went to a party together. I overheard my husband has been cheating on me. I held in the tears until we came home. I questioned him. He yelled at me. His eyes widened, and he hit me. He scared my son and me. Then, we went to sleep.

The next day, we went to counseling. The male counselor seemed to side with my husband for cheating. The counselor told me to drop out of college. I refused. The car ride was silent, and I refused to talk to my husband. His eyes changed appearing wider.

He grew angry after the conversation at counseling. I questioned him about the girl. The phone rang numerous times. I answered it, and a young girl asked for my husband. He told me to go upstairs with my son, which was suspicious. I hid by the stairway, listening.

I cried after he hung up the phone, "How could you? I love you so much. I bought you a car and did everything for you. My family pays your bills."

He kept hitting me and kicking me in front of my son. I was black-and-blue. He left and stated he had work. I did not believe him, and at that point, I did not care.

I called up my grandma for help. The mail with my grandma's money came. I waited an hour and took my son's and my clothing in bags. My son and I left Delaware quickly. We took a cab to Wilmington, and then two trains until we arrived in Long Island. I was in tears. I bought my son food along the way. My son was so well-behaved during our traveling. I had to do what was best for my son and me.

# CHAPTER SEVENTEEN

## A Chemical Imbalance

I never smoked cigarettes and never took drugs. I never went to bars and drank alcohol. I never went to dance clubs or stripper places. I was always the outcast in the crowd. Things I enjoyed were bowling, movies, eating out, reading clinical psychology books, and shopping for clothes. I guess I am a boring bookworm nerd. I love being a mother to my son. I went always to the library every day to read books and do massive research.

Before being diagnosed with mild paranoid schizophrenia, I had some horrifying experiences. It started at the end of my fourth year in college. I was twenty-one years old at that time. Experiencing hallucinations and delusions were scary. I did not understand what was happening to me. I saw shadows of imaginary people chasing me. At that time, I was living with my grandma in New York City. I was scared to tell my mother.

Socially, I would withdraw from people. Every time, I went to college, I wrote letters to my professor stating, "Someone is following me. I must leave class fast." I ran like a lightning to take a cab to Grandma's apartment to hide inside my bed. I felt that was my only safe place. I was shaking and scared and not knowing what was going on with me.

Most of my hallucination breaks were triggered by my ex-husband who abused me. Before getting diagnosed, I had sleeping problems. I did not sleep for a week. I started hearing voices, and put wrapping paper on the windows to hide from the shadows of people. I did not know that I was hallucinating. I was scared. Every night, I had frightening dreams. I did not sleep for approximately one week, feeling utterly weak and withdrawn.

My mother called her friend who was a nurse. My mother's friend took me to the hospital. The doctor did an evaluation on me asking numerous questions. They took away my platform shoes and hairclip because of other patients. Some patients were dangerous and suicidal and refused their treatment. I was not aware of what was going on.

There was a nurse who got my address information, my date of birth information, and my first and last name to put into the computer. She had puffy and static hair. All I could recall was laughing a lot because I was not aware what was going on before being on medication and being diagnosed. I called the lady "a clown." Basically, I was hallucinating, not aware of what was going on.

The doctors asked me about my medical history and being abused. I was transferred to another hospital to get diagnosed. I cried inside the ambulance. I did not know what was going on. I was tired. When I arrived at another hospital, I was scared. I cried to go home, not knowing anything about my diagnosis. I sat at the desk for intake. The male nurse asked me questions. I felt light-headed and dizzy. I fainted in front of the male nurse onto the floor. I was lying on the floor, feeling weak. The male nurse squeezed an alcohol pad near my nose. He picked me up to sit back onto the chair and handed me orange juice. The orange juice brought up my sugar level. My blood pressure was low. The nurses took lot of tubes of blood from my arm. My arm was hurting.

The male nurse said, "Have you been eating because you look tiny? Have you been sleeping?"

I said crying, "I eat one meal a day because my husband wants me to stay anorexic. My husband abused me, and I have an order of protection. I want to divorce my husband. I have not been sleeping for a week because I can't sleep."

The male nurse felt sorry for me and told me to remain strong. I was scared in the hospital. As part of the routine procedures are the nurse checks for drug testing, too.

I cried, "You are going to hurt my arm. I do not take drugs."

They also weighed me on the scale. I weighed ninety pounds at the age of twenty-one.

After hours later, I was diagnosed with mild paranoid schizophrenia. I explained to the doctors in the hospital that I must go home to pursue my dreams being a productive person in the workforce. I was an art teacher. I also wanted to go home to my mother and my son.

I asked the doctors for some paper and a pen to write my college assignments. I sat in the corner of my hospital room at a desk. As I was crying, I was determined to be productive while I got treated medically. I decided to write my bachelor's thesis and history of religion final exam. My thesis was based on my life's experiences in relation to my artwork. I used art history in comparison. I just wanted to be left alone by other patients. I was in my own little studying world. *I am a bookworm.*

My mother did not visit me at the hospital except for once. It made me upset inside and lonely. Other patients had their families. I felt like a crap, and cried seeing other patients getting visitors. All I did was, sat in the room and read books and wrote poetries, *and cried . . .*

During the hospital process, I remained in contact with my lawyer about getting a divorce. She stated to me, just take your medication and remain stable so you can go back to work as an art teacher, etc. I listened to my lawyer's encouragement. I am grateful for her emotional support.

For a week, I had a schedule to follow in the hospital. There was group therapy, recreational therapy, music and games, and medication management. I took my medication everyday and went to the therapy sessions. I got discharged to home to see my mother and my son. I went to outpatient therapy and medication management once a month. My doctor put me on Risperdal for a year, and I had side effects. I did not get my period for a year and gained thirty-five pounds; I had to wear glasses permanently as a side effect of the medication. My eyes were sensitive to light now.

In 2002, I was put on a small dose of Abilify and a small dose of Seroquel. These particular medications helped me to live a productive life. (Note: Not every medication works for everyone.) I was able to work, finish college, and take care of my son as a single parent. I remained on my medication everyday and went to therapy once a month.

Being in the hospital was a nightmare and scary. I was stuck with other patients who had worse condition than me. Some patients tried to break the windows, which were barred up. Some patients were tied up in restraints, while others were locked in a time-out room. There were patients who were homeless and straight from jail. Patients were refusing to take their medications.

I could not take the chaos, and I remained medically stable and listened to the doctors. I had no more relapses and no more hallucinations. I was told it will be just a diagnosis of mild paranoid schizophrenia, once I am stable on my medication everyday. Again, note that not every medication works for everyone with the same diagnosis. Every day, I cried to go home. I was discharged quickly by doctors. I never saw a dangerous, scary place. It was a horrifying experience. I was mad at my mother for a long time for forcing me to go to the hospital. It was hard to forgive her. I could have been evaluated by an outpatient clinic instead of being stuck in a hospital. Still, to this day, I go to an outpatient doctor, only for medication management to remain stable and have a normal life.

*If I was ever to lose a job because of discrimination based on using my diagnosis against me,* I will sue them. *I am a hard worker, who is very educated and responsible.*

I have been released from a job in the past at a school district due to my disability, and I got the Division of Human Rights involved. The school district pretended I never did my job to cover up being prejudice about my diagnosis. I would come home crying everyday from work, and I was treated badly by workers inside the school district. The Division of Human Rights was going to either get my job back or make me unemployed. I refused to work for people who were prejudice and treated me bad. I took the unemployment instead, and waited two years for another teaching job and got it. I am very happy with my current head teaching job.

# CHAPTER EIGHTEEN

## Researching My Diagnosis

While taking clinical psychology classes in college, I have learned a lot. I would question myself who in hell would have schizophrenia, bipolar, ADHD, etc. I laughed it off. Sure enough, I have mild paranoid schizophrenia. No two people are alike with the diagnosis of any brain disease or medical problems when responding to treatment. Many people can successfully manage their symptoms and are able to live quite well. Some patients need lifelong support. This can include hospitalization. People do not recognize their own illness, and a person doesn't know when they are hallucinating.

Schizophrenia is one of the most common mental illnesses. The disease begins between the ages of fifteen and twenty-five. Men and women are affected equally. Very rarely, symptoms appear before the age of twelve.

Paranoid schizophrenia is a frequent auditory hallucination of one or more delusions. If one is not taking their medications everyday and have this diagnosis, you can have a relapse. The symptoms that I experienced were: confusion, inability to think clearly, inability to pay attention or concentrate, hearing voices, and seeing objects or people that don't exist. It was hard for me to fight through all the chaos hallucinations, and I struggled to complete my schooling before being diagnosed paranoid schizophrenia.

Before doctors arrive at a diagnosis of schizophrenia, they do a psychiatric evaluation. There is a physical exam, a mental status exam, and a blood test. The doctors observe the patient's behavior, movement, mood, and sensory perceptions. Doctors also check for social or occupational problems to rule out other illnesses.

There is no answer what causes schizophrenia. Schizophrenia is heredity, meaning it runs in the families. A viral infection during pregnancy may increase chances of a child developing schizophrenia later in life. Also a chemical imbalance of the brain chemicals like dopamine, glutamate, and serotonin may cause schizophrenia. People with schizophrenia have abnormal brain structure and function.

How is schizophrenia treated? Most people, for the first time, are treated in the hospital. Psychiatrists interview the patient. Doctors keep a close eye on the patient for medication side effects. It takes a while for symptoms to be controlled. After discharged, the patient joins an outpatient program for treatment. The patient sees a social worker and psychiatrist for medication management.

Medications help eliminate psychotic symptoms. It works to decrease the chemical imbalance, which is causing symptoms. Everyone's body is different to metabolize medication. It can take months to find the right dose or medication. If you stop taking medications prescribed by your psychiatrist, you will have a relapse. Stick with your treatment plan and medications! Paranoid schizophrenia is a lifelong disease. People with schizophrenia will need special medical care and medication for their whole lives.

# CHAPTER NINETEEN

## My Accomplishments

After missing a week of college, I went back to college and handed in my bachelor's thesis and history of religion final exam. I spoke to the chairman of the fine arts department and explained why I missed a lot of college. The chairman was very nice and accepting. I revealed my diagnosis to him, and he stated that I was brave. He was very understanding and supportive.

In June 2002, I received my graduation letter, and it was held at Lincoln Center in New York City. I was excited and cried. My mother and grandma were proud of me.

My mother and grandma said, "You are graduating. You did it."

The day before graduation, my mother and I went out to a dress shop and bought a nice, long blue gown. I bought black shoes. I was planning to wear pink lipstick and blue eye shadow. We went to the salon to get an updo hairstyle with one curl hanging in front of my face to look sexy.

My mother, my son, and I took the Ronkonkoma train to Penn Station, New York. It was a slow train ride; the train stopped at every stop, one hour and forty minutes long. I was feeling nervous and restless wearing my elegant gown. My son was so well-behaved on the train. When we arrived at Penn Station, we took a cab to Lincoln Center. We made good timing. I was the first one there.

As we went inside Lincoln Center, it was huge and beautiful. We went up many flights of stairs. It was making me tired. My mother and son went on a separate line for a seat. The students were grouped within their majors and their degrees. It was well organized. Each student was called up one at a time by their major and their degree onto the huge stage. There were college photographers taking pictures of each graduate. They handed us the pictures at the end of the stage. I was grateful for the pictures.

After the graduation was over, I saw my best friend Jay in the hallway. I introduced Jay to my son and my mother. My mother took a picture of both of us together. We were both glad to graduate. Then, we all went outside to line up to collect our bachelor's degree. We hung outside for a little while and talked. My family and I ate out to celebrate.

I accomplished a lot in a short time period. I loved taking clinical psychology classes and aced them. I aced my history of religion final exam paper that I did in the hospital. I received a good grade on my bachelor's thesis paper. When you put your mind to things, anything can happen. Keep dreaming, and never stop dreaming. Believe in yourself even when others do not, just reach for the stars.

I have a certification in CPR and First Aide. I have a certificate in Teacher Aide. I have a NY State Teacher Assistant License K-12 grade. I enjoy teaching particularly in preschool and elementary levels.

Participating in small art exhibitions make me happy. In August 2009, I won Honorable Mention at Stony Brook Museum for my artwork called "Fire Island." I love painting pictures, drawing, writing poetry, and photography.

I taught art to grades K-12—fine arts and art history. I taught in a day care for two years, but I was discriminated for revealing my diagnosis. If I ever need a special accommodation at a job, I get discriminated for my disability. I get let go. It is hard trying to get a job on Long Island, but I never give up. Some people are narrow-minded when they hear someone has a disability. It is not right. There is no one perfect in this world.

I received many scholarships toward my undergraduate classes; for example, SADD scholarship, School of Visual Arts Merit scholarship, Veterans scholarship, and POW/MIA scholarship. My GPA was a 3.5, and I was an Honor Society student. I did internships in art education, teaching K-12 grade in New York City and on Long Island.

Currently, I am taking care of my son who has ADHD (attention deficient hyperactive disorder). He takes medications everyday to function well. He is sports oriented and MVP of all his sports.

I am a head teacher at a day care teaching toddlers. I really enjoy my job; it is a rewarding job. I also currently go to graduate school for my master's degree in early childhood birth through second grade, and so far my GPA is a 3.0. My goal is to remain as a head teacher either in a day care center or in a preschool setting.

# CHAPTER TWENTY

## Moving from NYC Back to Long Island

After college graduation, reality comes to an end. I did not ride anymore in luxury cabs, no more bus and train rides. I had to drive myself in a car all over Long Island. Grandma and I moved back to my mother's house on Long Island. At the age of seventy-six, my grandma could not live by herself anymore. She had a massive heart attack. I was scared. She was forced to retire her full-time job as a maid in New York City. She worked seven days a week like a beaver to help my son and me financially.

Packing all my clothing, paintings, and sculptures was a nightmare. I felt stressed and overwhelmed. There were boxes after boxes, packing them carefully. It took me two days to pack up my belongings. The moving truck came to pick up our stuff to be transported to my mother's house.

Good-bye, New York City. Hello, back to Long Island. I was crying. I loved living in New York City. In New York City, I loved the crowds, the luxury cabs, the museums, the art galleries, shopping for clothes, and the cultural diversity. It felt like luxury. Not to mention, the millions of men in New York City look gorgeous wearing their business suits.

My grandma and I spent a lot of time together. There were times we bickered about what to eat for dinner and my relationship, my boyfriend. That is natural. My grandma always wanted the best for me. When I felt depressed, my grandma and I cried together; she tried to cheer me up. My grandma never turned her back on me.

Back on Long Island, my Grandma and my son played a lot racing cars across the kitchen floor. They sang and laughed together. My grandma helped to feed my son and clothed him. She was a great person. Not too many grandmas in this world like mine.

My grandma said to my son, while feeding him, "Here's the airplane. Zoom."

My son laughed. He ate very well with a big appetite. My son was a messy eater and still is today. My son loves food.

Unpacking my belongings from grandma's apartment was very annoying. It took me a week to get everything organized. I had to buy another bookshelf. I had two hundred books from art books to clinical psychology books. I placed my paintings inside my walk-in closet. My computer came back damaged. Some of my abstract sculptures broke; I had to throw it out. I hung up my clothes in the closet and put the rest of my clothing in my dresser. I love having lot of clothes.

I am a full-time mother and dedicated. I did not need a babysitter anymore. I love taking care of my son. He is my world. It was heartbreaking not seeing my son when he first crawled and first walked during my college years. My son looked like a cute newborn monkey when he learned to walk. My son's first word was "Mom." My son has a beautiful smile and is very photogenic.

# CHAPTER TWENTY-ONE

## My Grandma Passed Away

On April 1, 2006, I started to feel empty, emotionally. My grandma looked old and sick. She was playing on the rug with my son. My son's cars and Ninja Turtle figures were scattered around the floor. They were laughing and talking to each other. It was cute. My grandma and my son loved each other so much. They also colored together in a coloring book.

My grandma and I also had a conversation while she played with my son. We talked about, hoping I meet a nice guy in the future, getting my book published, and finding a well-paid job. My grandma and I were close like peas and carrots. She would call me her "shadow."

My grandma said, "I am going upstairs to make coffee."

My grandma fell down the stairs. I ran to my grandma like lightning.

I cried, "Grandma, are you okay?"

She started babbling like a baby, not speaking. I called my mother first at her job and told her the situation. I dialed 911 and called the ambulance right away. I had my grandma sit on the couch until the EMTs arrived. They took an awful long time. Then, my mother arrived home.

The EMT came slowly. The EMT man asked what happened. I explained to the EMT my grandma fell down the stairs. I touched her head; there was a small bump on her head. The EMT man took Grandma's blood pressure. He had a hard time getting my grandma's attention and stated your grandma is now blind in both eyes. My grandma was still babbling like a baby, and I could not make out any word. The EMTs took my grandma to the hospital. My mother, my son, and I followed the ambulance to the hospital.

At the hospital, the doctors and nurses took many tests on my grandma. The first test my grandma went through was a computed tomography of the brain. It is x-rays of the brain that can show whether there's bleeding. The next test my grandma went through was a MRI. An MRI finds out the amount of damage to the brain and helps to predict possible recovery.

She also took blood tests. The blood tests results tell the doctors the blood sugar, the electrolytes, and the liver and kidney function. The nurse put IV inside my grandma's arm. She had to be tied to the bed in restraints in the hospital. She was trying to constantly get out of the hospital bed. It was upsetting to watch my grandma.

Hours and hours passed; the results showed my grandma had three massive strokes. A stroke is life-threatening damage in which parts of the brain are deprived of oxygen. The strokes caused my grandma to go blind. She had no control on anything. My grandma could not feed herself and had to wear adult diapers. It was heartbreaking.

My grandma smoked a pack of cigarettes a day. This could double the risk of having a stroke. My grandma did not eat healthy. She loved to eat candy (chocolate), cookies, cakes, cereal for supper, and sometimes meats. My grandma's favorite chocolate was Russell Stover. My grandma should have eaten fish, vegetables, meats, and salads. She had high cholesterol and was on medication. Later on, my grandma lost her eyesight, too.

My grandma was transferred to a nursing home. She was on IV and still not eating. My mother's decision was to put a feeding tube inside my grandma. Visiting my grandma and seeing her helpless was unbearable. She would sleep a lot and hold onto a doll and called it baby after my son. My grandma really loved us, especially my son.

On April 2, 2006, the nursing home called our house. I answered the phone. I told the nurse my mother is at work and asked what was wrong.

I said, "Is my grandma, okay?"

The nurse said, "The last word your grandma said was 'baby.' I am sorry, she passed away."

I cried. I asked for the nursing home's phone number and told the nurse I will have my mother call back.

I called my mother up as an emergency at work. I broke the bad news to my mother. My mother cried and started yelling at me. It was a disaster. My grandma had no life insurance, and my mother struggled to pay for my grandma's wake, the burial, and her name engraved on the stone. My grandma was buried in Queens, New York, and the wake was on Long Island. I was too upset to go to her burial, but I went to the wake. It was hard seeing my grandma lying in a coffin and a room filled with only five people who showed up to pay their respects. Meanwhile, my grandma was a good mentor, a hard worker, and helped many people. People were crying, and I held in my emotions. I waited until I came home and cried in my bedroom.

My son and I were sad when grandma passed away, too. She was eighty years old, and I was hoping she would have made one hundred. My grandma was my angel who looked over me. I am very grateful to have a good Grandma in my life. My grandma is always in my thoughts. There is not another Grandma like mine in this world. I loved and respected my grandma. I will always remember her for all the things she has taught me and done for me.

If my grandma was still alive, she would be proud of my accomplishments.

# CHAPTER TWENTY-TWO

## Divorced

In December 2005, I officially became divorced. Through years of therapy, I became strong as an individual. I took being abused, mentally and physically, by my ex-husband for too long. He would call me by horrible names like mental retard, bitch, you are fat, and Leslie. He even put liquid aftershave into a travel-size Scope bottle and laughed when it burned my mouth. I begged him to sign the divorce papers and drove him to the law firm. It was hard emotionally because he was my first love. I cried when we signed the divorce papers. It was over, at least I thought!

The day of the divorce, I took my husband out to Friendly's for our last meal together and paid for him. I was in tears and talked a little bit with him. I gave my husband two chances, and he failed to go to counseling for help. I tried everything. After our meal, I drove him back to his mother's house.

I was in and out of court for three years. It cost me approximately $20,000. It was a long process, but worth it. Going to court can drain you mentally, emotionally, and financially! The best part is we did not own a house. We did not have joint accounts because I did not want it. I owned nothing on purpose. I have my son living with me. My son means everything to me; he is my life.

My ex-husband was spiteful and called the authorities on me. He would make false allegations against me. The cases would be dropped with no findings. He would purposely have the court papers not sent to me properly. I would never receive the court papers. He tried to have me arrested for not knowing to show up for court. He loves to lie and cause trouble. He loves to see me upset crying. I could never forgive anything my ex-husband has put us through. I remained strong for my son and went to see a counselor to get through this disaster.

On November 2008, he came to my son's school to try to kidnap him. My ex-husband must have followed me without me knowing. I requested for my son to go to school away from our town, approximately ten minutes away from our house. I am sometimes scared for my son's safety because of my ex-husband.

On October 31, 2009, my son and I went to the mall for trick-or-treating. My son dressed up as human hotdog and looked cute. As we were walking, my ex-husband happened to be there and walked up close to my face. My son ran away frightened, and I froze like a deer in headlights. I did not know what to do. He kept calling my son by another name that was not his name. "I have been watching over you both a lot," he said.

I ran away with my son in the mall, and my ex-husband followed me.

"Stop . . . You are scaring us. You use to abuse us and hit us," I said.

He stopped following us. My son had a lot of anxiety and was scared.

# CHAPTER TWENTY-THREE

## A Letter to My Son

September 28, 2009<br>Typed at 12:00 a.m.

Dear Son,

I am blessed with you. I love you so much. Mommy struggles each and every day, but somehow we make it through the days. When you were born, I thought I was going to lose you from a low heart rate. You always pulled through, and I prayed for you. Angels where watching over us above. I would not know what I would do without you.

You were my little four-pound eleven-ounce chicken. I dressed you up in cute outfits as a baby. You had firefighter outfits, a cow outfit, a chicken outfit, suits, and many more. You are spoiled and also fed well.

When I came home from college and saw you walk and crawl, it made me have happy tears. You are my special boy. Every week, I came home from college, I bought you a new outfit in New York City. You are constantly on my mind.

When you were two years old, I took you to college with me. You played ball in the art studio room with the students for a little while when I had to get my artwork. You were so well-behaved. Then, I took you to my psychology class. My professor loved you and stated you are an active baby. You would draw pictures as I was learning in college.

The scariest thing I had to face with you was when you had a seizure. It was 2:00 a.m. and my mother saved you. My mother took you to the hospital, and the nurses and doctors took good care of you while I was coming home from college. I rushed to get to the hospital with Great-Grandma, Josephine. I would sleep in the hospital beside you in a chair. I was a nervous wreck. After a week, you were fine and returned home. I thought I was going to lose you again. You always pulled through for me.

You were in the best preschools on Long Island. Your first word was "Mom." You spoke in full sentences when you were three years old with the help of a speech therapy. You liked preschool. The teachers loved you, too. You were always well-behaved in school. You loved playing on the playground and making art.

At the age of three, you started on a bowling team with bumpers. Each year, after that, I had you join bowling. You received a medal and a trophy. I was so proud of you, and your average was 120. You loved getting spares and strikes. You took the game very seriously.

When you are five years old, you started kindergarten. I remember when you were in a play called *The Mitten* by Jan Brett. You were a little mouse in the play and dressed up in gray pants and a gray shirt. You were shy and spoke soft during the play. It made me cry tears of happiness. I was so proud of you.

The hardest thing in life for me was when you were evaluated at the doctors for ADHD. Always stay on your medications to live a productive life. It was heartbreaking. I take very good care of you. You are always at the doctors for your sick and well visits, plus your shots.

In second grade, I put you into Boy Scouts. We made crafts together, visited a bakery shop, and went on a nature walk. We made a wooden race car together and competed in a Boy Scout race. You came in third place. It was fun, and I was proud of you.

At the age of seven, I put you into full-contact football. You were a wide receiver and ran the ball like lightning. No one could catch you and touchdown. You loved football. You received your first most valuable player trophy. You were so excited.

During the spring season of 2008, you joined baseball. You became a first basemen and a lefty pitcher, sometimes. You would hit the baseball over the fence. I cheered for you and the team like a cheerleader. Then, one baseball coach heard about your baseball talent. You were asked to play in a summer travel baseball team.

The coach said, "It is rare to find a lefty who is talented at baseball."

During the summer baseball travel team, you played as a first basemen and sometimes a pitcher. At the end of the season, there was a baseball tournament. You played with passion and had your game face on. You received three MVP medals. I was happy for you and excited. I took pictures of you for memories. That's my boy!

In August 2008, you played full-contact football as a wide receiver and a lineman. It was a good season. You scored nine touchdowns. You tackled a lot of football players. At the end of the season, you received a MVP trophy, again. You are very talented in sports. Never give up sports, it will be your ticket to college and possibly more.

In January 2008, you started playing basketball. You threw every ball almost into the hoop. You played fairly, sharing the ball and helped taking it to the net. You would score the points for the team. You received a basketball trophy and played in the all-star basketball game. Your team won second place.

In April 2009, you played baseball again and voted the most valuable player. You played in Yaphank, New York, and received another trophy. It was an honor for you, and I am so proud of your achievements. It gave me chills in my body hearing your name announced on the loudspeaker for your trophy.

In May 2009, you joined the summer baseball travel team. It was a fabulous season. Baseball was thrice a week, plus games each week. There were doubleheader games, too. It was competitive. You played mainly first base and a couple of times as a pitcher. The team came in first place in divisional and runners-up in the tournament. You received a MVP trophy and a runners-up trophy. I was proud of you how hard you worked.

In September 2009, you joined full-contact football and soccer. In football, you are amazing linemen. You hold your ground and do well. You recover fumbles and make me proud. I am always there for you, cheering on the sidelines. I am probably the loudest mom running up and down the field, cheering.

In soccer, you are a wonderful goalie and catch almost every soccer ball. Keep up the good work. I am always on the sidelines cheering you on and saying, "The soccer ball is coming your way."

After the soccer game, you always tell me, "I know, Mom."

That soccer season, your team came in first place and won the championship. I took many pictures of you and the team. Also during fall 2010, my son helped his soccer team as a goalie and won the championship and received two trophies.

I had you attend a Catholic religion class to express our spirituality and belief in God. You had your baptism at a church on Long Island. You made your Communion at the age of eight.

You always do well in school, and I always will help you with your schoolwork. You have potential and intelligence like me. You joined chorus and have a sweet voice. You also have a heart of gold like me. You have a lot of good qualities inside you, just like me. Don't ever change. You are a well-rounded person. Always remember me by all the things, I have done for you.

**Love, Your Mother, Danielle Sparacio**

# CHAPTER TWENTY-FOUR

## Epilogue

September 28, 2009

Dear Diary,

I had so many heartbreaks and tragedies in my life. Sometimes, I can't cry no more. I remained strong and strived for excellence. I never stopped believing in myself.

Charles Darwin quoted, "Survival of the fittest." I had become a survivor of domestic violence, a survivor of a brain disease, and being pregnant as a teenager. I strived to graduate college and made it. Everything was overwhelming at times. Somehow, I got through it each day with the help of therapy. I stayed strong for my son.

Being a parent is wonderful. I love seeing my son grow up becoming a young little man. He has perseverance overcoming his disabilities. Just because one has a disability, it does not mean one can't do anything in life. People need to be less discriminating and more understanding. We have feelings, too.

I love helping people who are less fortunate than me. I donate clothing to the Goodwill. I, sometimes, donate canned food to the needy. I promise to keep volunteering at a museum on Long Island.

I want to always make sure my son is well-rounded. I will always help my son in every way. I would love to see my son go to college in the future and pursue baseball. I will help my son to strive to achieve good grades in school. We will always stay family-oriented.

In the future, I hope to buy my son and me a condo on Long Island. That will be my son's and my dream together.

Every day a person can learn something new. Everybody has different responsibilities. Nothing in life is guaranteed. I learned that quickly. For example, a woman is wearing a huge diamond wedding ring; it does not mean she is in the greatest marriage. The couple could be miserable, cheating on each other, or having financial problems and hate each other. My old diamond wedding ring is just a piece of scrap metal now from all the torment I went through.

There are signs to look for being in a domestic violent relationship. Here are examples I have been through: being put down or insulted me, he called me by names like mental retard, stupid, etc. He cursed at me and mocked me whatever I did, and told me what to wear. He tried to control me by preventing me from working, and I could not have any friends. He used to hit and kick me. Being with an abuser can be dangerous. Don't stay with someone who abuses you, there is help out there for women.

If a person hides their pain, it only gets worse. Some people slightly smile and make a few word conversations. The worst thing to do is not to hold back your emotions. Don't be someone else, just be who you are. And feel good about yourself. I wish everyone peace, love, and happiness. Follow your dreams and never give up. Things take time.

# AFTERWORD

On October 5, 2009, I turned thirty. I thought that I would never live to see my thirtieth birthday. I suffered for a long time with anorexia from the age of twelve to twenty-three. Through therapy and having a wonderful son, I have changed my life around. I battled having anorexia. I'd spent a lot of time reading Clinical Psychology books and reading *Psychology Today* magazines. I did a lot of research on my illnesses and went to get medical help. I also researched my son's illnesses, too.

My thirtieth birthday was a highlight of my life. My mother, my son, and I went to New York City. We all went to a museum on the west side of Manhattan. At the museum, we saw the different culture center, the monkeys, and the birds. My son loved the gift shop for his rock collection. We all went to eat at Carmine's restaurant on Ninetieth Street and Broadway. The plates of mixture seafood spaghetti Italian food were huge. It tasted delicious. I do recommend Carmine's to eat. My mother, my son, and I went clothes shopping. I felt like a teenager all over again. We rode in cabs all day. It was like luxury! I had the best thirtieth birthday.

Before getting divorced, I tried my hardest to work through my marriage with counseling, but it did not work. My ex-husband felt he did not need the help when he was abusing me. You cannot lead a horse to the cart. I deeply love my ex-husband, but still have in the back of my mind the "hell" he put us through. My therapist always reminds me that being abused by someone is not love. There is a part of me that still loves my ex-husband. There are days I feel sad inside and miss my ex-husband. I know my ex-husband will never change and I cannot go back. I can only move on forward in my life.

As far as my college education at School of Visual Arts is concerned, I was very satisfied. I learned a lot from college and applied everything I learned to the real world. The professors, financial aid department, art education department, and fine art department were outstanding.

I focus my energy and life all toward my son. We do homework together. I take my son to his sports games. I did not expect always to be a single parent throughout my life. There are times, I wish I could meet a guy and fall deeply in love and get married. I was so torn up inside from my ex-husband emotionally that it is hard to love another person that deeply again.

www.ingramcontent.com/pod-product-compliance
Lightning Source LLC
Chambersburg PA
CBHW020348290526
45785CB00005B/2190